2/-6

COWS AND COWBOYS
Yesterday and Today

by **IRENE** and **LAURENCE SWINBURNE**

illustrated by **RAY BURNS**

 A Finding-Out Book

PARENTS' MAGAZINE PRESS·NEW YORK

SOME OTHER FINDING-OUT BOOKS

Library of Congress Cataloging in Publication Data

Swinburne, Laurence.
    Cows and cowboys.

    (A Finding-out book)
    Includes index.
    SUMMARY: Traces the history of cowboys in the
West and describes their work and day-to-day life.
    1. Cowboys—The West—Juvenile literature.
2. The West—History—Juvenile literature.
[1. Cowboys—The West. 2. The West—History]
I. Swinburne, Irene, joint author.   II. Burns,
Raymond, 1924-   III. Title.
F596.S945   978   76-3442
ISBN 0-8193-0839-0

Contents

As I was a-walking one morning for pleasure,
I spied a young puncher riding along,
His hat was throwed back and his spurs were a-jingling,
As he approached me a-singing this song:
"Whoopee, ti-yi-yo, git along little dogies,*
It's your misfortune and none of my own,
Whoopee, ti-yi-yo, git along little dogies,
For you know Wyoming will be your new home."

—Old cowboy song

*Cowboys often called cattle "dogies."

Spanish Beginnings

There were no cattle or horses in the Americas before Columbus's three small ships sailed from Spain. Once there had been horses, but these had died out thousands of years before.

A few years after Columbus discovered America, 300 Spanish soldiers entered what is now the United States from Mexico. They were prepared to stay many months, perhaps even years. They had brought many Indians, cattle, and horses.

A few months before, the Spanish had heard a strange story from some Indians. They were told that there were seven cities north of Mexico where the houses and even the streets were made of gold.

It seems strange now that the Spanish would believe such a tale. But they had found riches in Mexico. Why wouldn't there be more?

They found no cities and they found no gold. After many months of wandering in the southwestern part of our country, they returned to Mexico tired and disgusted.

But they had left behind something far richer than the gold they were seeking. During the

journey, their cattle—long-horned cows—and horses wandered away. Sometimes the animals had been frightened by thunderstorms and had run off into the hills. Now and then young calves and colts had not been able to keep up with the soldiers, and there was no time to go back for them.

Though there were no cities of gold in the American plains, it was fine land for the cattle and horses the Spanish had left behind. There was enough grass and water to keep them alive, and in a few years thousands of these animals roamed over the plains.

Spaniards again came to this area, not to search for gold, but to settle. They were delighted to see the wild cattle. Soon herds of cows were being raised on the Spanish ranches of Texas. The newcomers used these long-horned cattle for milking and plowing. They didn't think the cow was useful for anything else.

Much, much later cattle of the southwest
United States would provide meat for the country.
The horses would be needed to bring those cows
to market. The man on horseback driving these
herds would be known as a cowboy.

What the Spanish soldiers had brought to our
country was far more valuable than what they
found, even more valuable than what they would
have found if there had been seven golden cities.

American Beginnings

About 300 years after the search for the golden cities, the United States won a war against the country of Mexico, which was then much larger than it is now. That's because the United States took possession after the war of what is now most of the southwestern part of our country. The land the United States took is now the states of California, Nevada, Utah, Arizona, New Mexico, and parts of Colorado, Oklahoma, and Texas.

At the same time, people in the East began to develop a taste for beef. And Texas was the land of wild cattle called Longhorns—hundreds of thousands of them.

There was only one problem, but it was a big one. How were the Texans to get the cattle to market? No railroads existed at this time between Texas and the cities of the East. Not many cows could be put aboard ships.

The answer was to walk the cattle to the nearest railroads. At that time, the railheads, as they were called, were in Missouri at Kansas City and St. Louis. That was a long walk for the cows—1,000 miles or more. There was no easy road to follow, either. Rivers had to be crossed, hills climbed, and there were long stretches without water, and unfriendly Indians. The trip was known as the Long Drive.

If the Longhorns lived through all this, they would actually gain weight before they reached the market. Although they had walked a great distance, they thrived on the prairie grass of the trail. A lot of money could be made by taking cattle on the Long Drives, if the herd and the cowboys could reach the end alive.

One group of people was far from happy about the millions of Longhorns going north. These were the farmers who were pouring into the rich prairie lands of the West. They had two complaints.

First, the herds came over their farms, making wide paths through their crops. Here was a trampled field of wheat, there was a smashed plot of corn.

Second, and even worse, the Longhorns carried an illness that was called Texas fever. They didn't get the fever themselves, but they passed it on to other cows.

It was little wonder that farmers, looking at their ruined crops and dying cattle, shook their fists at the great moving herds. They did more than shake fists, too. They banded together and met the cowboys with guns ready. Angry words would be passed between them, and sometimes bullets, too. Now and then, the cattlemen would break through. More often, they paid money for any damage they did, or turned aside and went around the farms.

The farmers had another weapon, as well. They outnumbered the Texas cattlemen. Also, the farmers were citizens of the states the trail went through, and the Texans were not. Laws were passed against cattle drives going through certain areas. Drives in the future could only go west of these areas. Soon the Texas herds could not get into Missouri.

The Texans were lucky, though. The railroads were stretching west into Kansas. The Longhorns could now be brought to new railheads. Small towns became big overnight as the thundering herds came—towns few people had heard of up to that time, such as Wichita and Abilene, both in Kansas.

But the farmers from the East were still coming, too. And they still worried about their cows getting the Texas or tick fever, and about getting their crops stamped down. The government of Kansas made the Texans move their trails west, and still farther west. Now Ellsworth was the railhead. Then it was Dodge City.

The cattlemen from Texas realized they were in a war they had no chance of winning. There had to be some other way.

What if they moved their cattle ranges west of Kansas, to Colorado? Or north of Kansas to Nebraska, Wyoming, even Montana and Idaho?

The winters came sooner up there, lasted longer, and were much colder. "Sometimes," said Mark Twain, the famous writer, in talking about this north country, "we have winter all summer . . . "

But the Longhorn was a tough animal. It could live anywhere, as long as it had a little grass to munch on and a little water to drink.

All in all, raising cattle was—and still is—a ticklish business. A ranch owner might make a lot of money one year by driving a herd of nice, sleek, fat Longhorns to market. By the next year, the cattleman might be broke. A sudden blizzard might catch much of his herd out on the plains where they would freeze to death. Not even the rugged Longhorn could live through such biting cold and driving snow. Or Indians might run off with many of his best cows. Or more Longhorns might be raised than were needed. Then the cattleman would get only a low price for his herd.

The First Cowboys

The first American cowboys did not speak English. Besides, they were slaves—not black slaves, but Indians. They rode on ranges belonging to the Spanish owners in California and Texas, before there was a United States. Soon the Indians became better horsemen than their masters. They were called vaqueros (from *vaca*, a Spanish word meaning "cow").

It was against Spanish law to teach Indians to ride horses, but the government was at Mexico City, which was far away. So the Spanish landowners taught the vaqueros to ride because they needed men to take care of their large herds.

Many Americans came to Texas following the war with Mexico. When Easterners began to demand Texas beef, many vaqueros went to work on the new ranches, teaching their skills to the Texas cowboys.

The newcomers also picked up the vaqueros' Spanish words. Few Texas cowboys knew Spanish, however, and many of the words were changed. Here are a few of the vaquero words that the Texas cowboys took over:

Palomino

Spanish word	Which meant	Texas cowboys used this word
vaquero (*va*-care-o)	cowboy	buckaroo
chaperreras (cha-pe-*rare*-ras)	leather trousers	chaps
la reata (la-ree-*ah*-ta)	rope used to capture steers	lariat
lazo (*la*-zo)	another word for rope	lasso
mestango (me-*stan*-go)	wild or stray horse	mustang
broncho (*bron*-ko)	untamed horse	bronco
juzgado (haz-*gah*-dough)	jail	hoosegow
cincha (*sin*-sha)	strap attached to saddle that goes around horse's body	cinch
sombrero (som-*bray*-ro)	high pointed hat with a brim shaped like a saucer	sombrero
palomino (pa-lo-*mee*-no)	a horse of a cream color	palomino
pinto (*pin*-tow)	a spotted horse	pinto or paint

The Cowboy at Home

The Texas cowboy had two lives. For a good part of the summer he was "on the trail" taking cattle north to the railheads. Most of the year he worked on the home ranch.

The cowboy's year really started in the spring when he and the other cowboys went out on the roundup. For many months the cattle had been allowed to roam free on the ranch or out on the land that didn't belong to anyone. Often the ranch owner would team up with other owners in rounding up the cows. That way from 100 to 200 cowhands would work together in gathering the herds.

Each cowboy knew what adult cow or bull belonged to his ranch. The brand would tell him.

A brand was a special mark on the cow's hide.

A young cow, born since the last roundup, had to be branded. A cowboy would ride after the unmarked cow. His lasso, or lariat, would make a singing sound as he swung it above his head. At just the right moment—swish!—the rope would snap through the air and wind around the animal's horns.

That would stop the cow long enough for
another cowhand to toss his lariat around the
back legs. Now the Longhorn was down on the
ground, unable to move, as the two riders kept
their ropes tight.

A man on foot would run up with a red-hot branding iron and stamp it on the cow's back quarters. The cow was branded and nothing would erase that mark. Many people thought this was cruel. The cattlemen would answer that the brand was the only way they could think of to prove that certain cows were their property.

Here are some brands used by Texas ranches:

Sometimes wild cows with no brands would be found during the roundup. These were called mavericks. Any rancher could claim one as his own if he could catch and brand it.

A roundup might last as long as a month and the cowboys might ride hundreds of miles. They would not return to their ranch in that time. They would sleep outside in bedrolls. But many cowboys did not mind the roundup. It was then that they could meet with their friends from other ranches.

When the roundup was finished, the ranch owners would pick the fattest cows from their herd. These they would start back toward home. The rest they let go to live on the open range for more months until they were ready for market.

The Texas cowboy probably was glad to see the home ranch again, but he knew he would not stay there long. In a few days, he would be heading north with the herd on the way to a railhead in Kansas or Missouri.

He would not return until late summer, but even then he had no time for a vacation. There would be another roundup, this time to brand the calves that had been born during the summer.

A cowboy was lucky if he had a job for the winter. There wasn't much work around a ranch, then, and two out of every three cowhands were told to find jobs in town and come back in the spring.

What work there was
on the ranch, though,
could be hard—especially
climbing tall windmills
which provided water for
many ranches. These
windmills shook as the
wind tore by and the
blades whirled. A man
could—and sometimes did—
fall off to be hurt and
even killed.

There was one other winter chore cowboys did
not like much. On many very large ranches cabins
were built out on the open range. Here men
would be stationed to look after the cows in the
area. It was a very lonely job. One man to a
cabin was the rule, and many cowboys would
almost go out of their minds after weeks of not
talking to anyone.

Not that a cowboy didn't have enough to do at
the outpost cabin, especially if a hated blizzard,
called a "blue norther," happened to hit. The

snow would pile up and the streams would freeze solid. Then the cows would stand on the prairie helplessly without food or drink. The cowboy would have to find an area where the snow had blown off, and then lead the cows to it. While they munched the grass, he would have to chop holes in the ice so they could drink.

A man could not do such a job all winter. Sooner or later, the ranch owner or foreman would send out another person to take the place of the cowboy who had been there for two or three weeks. With a whoop, the freed cowboy would head back to the ranch headquarters—to his friends in the bunkhouse.

The bunkhouse was crowded and noisy, for all the cowboys lived there. But at least there was one place each cowboy could call his own—his bunk. There he kept all he owned in the world—his weapons, ropes, and saddle.

The bunkhouse was usually made of rough logs and the floors were dirt. The cowboys would put newspapers all over the walls to keep the house warm. In the spring, the dwelling became too warm and the men would sleep outside on the ground.

The Cowboy on the Long Drive

The Long Drive to bring the herd from Texas to the railheads was the most exciting part of the cowboy's life, and also the most boring. Days filled with riding in the dust raised by the Longhorns were dull and tiring. But other days the cowboys would never forget, days filled with danger.

Always on the day the drive started, there was a feeling of great excitement. The cowboys would stamp out of the bunkhouse for a quick breakfast, when the stars were still gleaming brightly. Then, as the sun rose, they would toss their bedrolls on the chuck wagon and mount their horses.

The trail boss, who would be in charge of the cowboys until the cattle were delivered, would give a shout. The cowboys would begin to move the herd. Certain steers that were leaders would be pushed ahead by yells. The rest of the herd would follow. They were on their way north.

The trail boss would ride ahead of the herd, stretching it out until the cows might form a line two or more miles long. In the rear would come the wrangler, a cowboy who took care of the extra horses, of which there might be as many as 80. The men would not ride the same horses all day for that would be too tiring for the animals. The wrangler would give them fresh mounts. The extra horses were called the *remuda*. Taking care of those extra horses was a thankless chore and usually the wrangler would be a young cowboy on his first drive.

Slightly ahead of the herd, but to the side of the trail, the chuck wagon would creak along. It was the food carrier and the cook drove it. The

trail boss was leader everywhere except here. Chuck wagon cooks tended to be crusty, taking no nonsense from anyone. If a cowboy happened to poke fun or play a practical joke on the cook, he might find himself on the receiving end of a pot of boiling water or a pan.

Plod, plod, plod all day, except for a short stop for lunch—that was the way of the Long Drive. At sunset, the trail boss would call a halt. They would have traveled from eight to twelve miles. The cook would dish out the meal—usually just fried bacon, beans, and coffee. The cowboys would squat by the side of the trail and eat.

Surprisingly enough, they rarely ate beef, although they were surrounded by cows. Beef cost too much.

After supper, the cowboys would sit around the fire. One might strum on his guitar or banjo, someone else would begin singing, and soon everyone would join in. Well, not quite everyone. Some men had to ride around the herd at all times.

This nightwatch prevented cows from wandering off and kept rustlers or Indians from taking away any cattle. Rustlers were men who made their living by stealing cows. They would lay another brand over the one on the cow's hide to make it appear that the cow belonged to another ranch. Only horse stealing was a worse

crime than cattle rustling in the Old West.

The nightwatch had to keep the cattle calm. Longhorns tended to be nervous animals, especially after dark. The cowboys would ride slowly and softly and sing—yes, actually sing—to the herd. Many so-called cowboy songs were really cow lullabies.

The greatest fear at night was a stampede. Anything might set it off—a flash of heat lightning, the hoot of an owl, a horse's whinny. The herd would take off like a shot and then the cowboys would dig their heels into their horses' flanks and go after them.

The chase might go on for miles. Finally a cowboy would pull in front of the thundering

animals. He would shoot his pistol once, twice, three times and pray that the Longhorns would stop. Usually they did, but many a young cowboy met his death under their hoofs.

The other cowboys who had been singing or sleeping would come up and help soothe the frightened cows until morning. Then they would make a rough count of the cattle. Usually this

would show that some animals had run away. That was bad enough, but even worse was the fact that the average cow had lost fifty pounds during the run! That meant less money for the ranch owner at the railhead.

River crossings presented a problem, too. Sometimes the rivers were smooth-running with gentle currents. The lead steers would plunge into the water. Then the rest of the herd and the cowboys would follow. At such times, it was not hard to swim across.

But if there had been a lot of snow on the mountains and it had melted, then the rivers would be high and raging. The lead steers would have to be forced into the swirling water. Even the cowboys weren't happy about such crossings. The currents were dangerous and quite a few men and horses were pushed over by the swift currents and drowned.

Most drives would cross through the Indian
Territory (now the state of Oklahoma). It was a
rare drive that wasn't stopped by Indians. After
some talk and hard bargaining, the trail boss
would cut out some cows from the herd and give
them to the warriors.

It is easy to understand the Indians' viewpoint.
Once they had hunted freely on these wide plains.
Now the great buffalo herds were being destroyed
and the Indians were being pushed into

reservations. Many Indians were starving. All they asked from the cowboys was a little food. If they didn't get it peacefully, they were prepared to fight for it. Anything was better than death.

After two or three months, the tired cowboys would lead the herd into the stockyards by a railroad. The trail boss would receive the money for the cattle. Then he would pay off the men. They might receive as much as $100 for almost a summer's work.

The cowboys would go into the nearest town where they spent a few days resting and celebrating. Then it was time to go home. Most would go by stagecoach because usually the horses had been sold with the cattle. The only cowboys to ride home would be those who had brought their own horses or bought them at the railhead.

Going up the trail was tough work that required a great deal of skill. It was hard work and badly paid. Yet to most Texas cowboys it was a great adventure.

Boots and Saddles: The Cowboy's Gear

Almost everything the cowboy owned he used in his job. He usually did not have much gear—only what he could carry easily from place to place on a horse.

He took great pride in his boots, hat, and saddle. The boots, often made especially for him, were soft leather and lambskin. They were not only foot coverings, they were tools. The pointed toes acted like fingers when the cowboy had to feel for the stirrups. Because of the high heels, the boot could not slip through the wide stirrup. They also helped him get a footing when he was on the ground trying to bring a roped cow to a halt. The boots were high to keep stones out and to protect the shins from thorns. The most prized boots were

those with fancy stitched designs, often in bright colors.

Most cowboys wore the sombrero, the tall and wide-brimmed hat. But sombreros might differ, depending on the area. In Texas and the states near the Mexican border, the brims were very wide to keep the blazing sun out of the cowboy's eyes. In the north cattle country of Colorado, Montana, and Wyoming, the sun did not glare as much and so the brims were not as wide. Some cowboys did not wear sombreros; they liked straw hats or derbies better.

The most valuable piece of equipment was the saddle. A cowboy would sell his guns, his sombrero, boots, even his horse, before he would bargain away his saddle. The cowboy saddle was first created by the vaqueros. Changes were made later, but it was always basically the vaquero saddle. The leather was set on a wooden frame. The horn was used as a hitching post for the cowboy's rope. When he lassoed a cow and had to dismount for branding, the rope attached to the horn would hold the cow fast. For easy riding, the cowboys on the prairie liked a low cantle—the back part of the saddle that supported the rider's

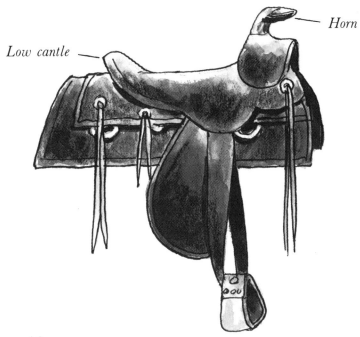

Horn

Low cantle

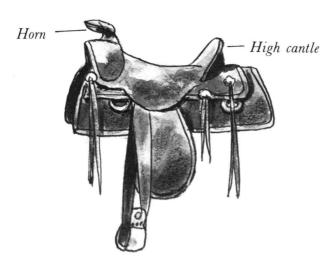

Horn —   — *High cantle*

back. But cowhands in mountain areas preferred a high cantle; it held them in the saddle when they were going uphill. A saddle weighed from 30 to 40 pounds.

The cowboy's chaps were more coveralls than trousers. He used them when riding because the Texas prairie was covered with prickly plants. The chaps, made of tough leather or animal skins

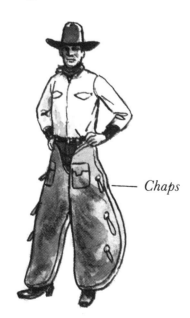

— *Chaps*

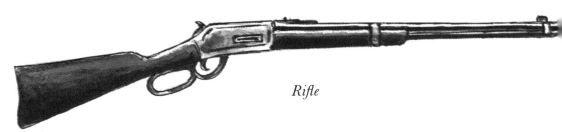

Rifle

protected the cowboy's real trousers and his legs.

The cowboy's weapons were his revolver, rifle, and a large knife. The revolver came in handy for stopping stampedes and for killing rattlesnakes. Even though TV and the movies show differently, cowboys were only fair marksmen. They didn't have time to practice shooting. Some ranch owners would not allow their cowhands to carry revolvers.

A cowboy seldom used a rifle, except when hunting, which was not often. Usually he left it in the bunkhouse when he was on the Long Trail or roundup because it got in the way of roping and riding. The knife was his most practical weapon since it could cut branches or ropes.

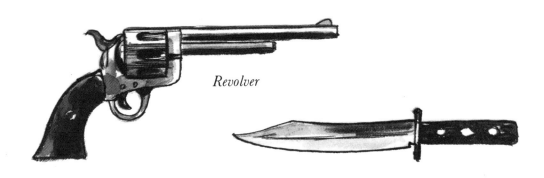

Revolver

Whenever he was at work, the cowboy had his rope. If he had the money, he bought a sixty-foot rawhide lariat. Rawhide was made from cow's skin, and was easy to throw. But most cowboys didn't have the cash for such a lasso. They made their own out of tough prairie grass.

All ropes had to be bent back and forth until they were flexible. However, if they became wet, they stiffened again.

Mustang

The Cowboy's Horses

A cowboy might own his horse, but he could not ride it all the time. It would be too tiring for the animal. The ranch owner provided him with other horses.

As you have seen, many horses were used in the Long Drive. Each cowboy was assigned seven or eight horses in the remuda. No other cowboy would use those horses.

Early in the days of the cattle industry, the Texas cowboys used the small wild horses of the

prairie—another gift that the Spanish explorers
had left when horses wandered away from their
small army. The animals liked Texas and in a few
years there were thousands of them.

In late spring the cowboys were ordered out on
the plains to catch mustangs—the wild horses.
They would take young but fully grown horses
about four years old and drive them back to the
ranch in the same way they drove cattle. The
ponies would be forced into a fenced-in area called
a corral. Then the bronco-buster would come.

Usually the buster would be a man who traveled from ranch to ranch, taming and training young horses. His was a dangerous job. He would have to lasso each horse and ride it. As the wild mustangs had never had a man on their backs, they bucked and twisted to rid themselves of the human burden. Sometimes the bronco buster would be hurled into the air and crash onto the ground, breaking his arm or leg.

When the mustang was trained, it was ready for

ranch work. Each horse would be skilled in at least one particular chore. Thus, one mustang might be used as a rope horse. On such a horse, a cowboy would dash after a cow, lariat twirling above his head. The horse would know just what speed was needed for the rider to make a good throw. When the rope tightened around the cow's horns, the horse would stop and dig its hoofs into the dirt. The roped animal would then come to a fast halt.

Another horse might be a good swimmer and be used when a river was reached on the Long Drive.

A night horse was a calm one that would be ridden on the nightwatch. This kind of horse would step gently and be careful not to excite the herd.

The smartest of all was the cutting horse. It would take years to train horses to this duty. A cutting horse would have to dive into a herd and cut out a particular cow or bull without scattering the others. It was tricky work for both horse and cowboy.

As ranches began to spring up in the northern states of Colorado, Wyoming, and Montana, other horses took the place of the mustang. The horse of the plains had been valuable on the Texas flatlands, but didn't do as well in colder climates and on mountain slopes. Here heavier horses were used.

Longhorn

Modern Cows and Cowboys

The Longhorn was a mighty cow indeed. For a long time, it was practically the only cow raised for beef in the United States. But cattlemen realized that other cows were better. These animals did not carry the dreaded Texas fever and they were fatter and more tender than the Longhorn. Slowly, but surely, other breeds began to appear on ranches until the Longhorn had almost disappeared.

Hereford

Bose Ikark, a black cowboy, saw Hereford cows at the Philadelphia World's Fair in 1876. This red and white animal was heavier than the Longhorn. Ikark could hardly wait to get back to Texas to tell his employer, Charles Goodnight, about this cow that had been developed in England. Soon the Whitefaces—as cowboys called the Herefords because they had white heads—were raised on the Goodnight ranch. The success that Goodnight had with the Herefords led other ranchers to buy

Shorthorn

them, too. Today, more Herefords are raised in the United States than any other beef cattle.

Shorthorn cattle was no newcomer to the United States. It had been raised in the East for nearly 100 years before it was introduced to western ranges. Easy to raise and heavier than most breeds, the Shorthorn is almost as popular as the Hereford. It can be either red, white, or a mixture of red and yellow.

Angus

The first Angus cow was brought from Scotland in 1873. Many people believe that this black short-legged animal produces the best meat.

Another popular beef cow is the Brahman—or the Zebus, as it is also called—which came to the United States from India on the other side of the world. This animal, which can be almost as black

Brahman

as the Angus, is well-suited to hot climates and can be found mainly in the South. However, its meat is not as tender as other brands. It is a strange-looking animal, having drooping ears and a small camel-like hump on its shoulders.

The Santa Gertrudis is the first beef cow developed in the United States. A mixture of the Shorthorn and the Brahman, this red cow is on an average 200 pounds heavier than other beef cattle.

These animals replaced the Texas Longhorn in a short time. By 1925 there were only 3,000 Longhorns left in the United States. These were mainly used in western movies.

Santa Gertrudis

But today, this brown, lanky cow with horns
that can extend nine feet from tip to tip is
making a comeback and for a very good reason.
The other breeds are fattened on grain. Grain has
become very costly and depends on the weather.
The Longhorn gains weight by eating grass, and
there is plenty of that in the West.

The cowboy's life has changed, too. The
modern cowhand certainly has an easier life than
the cowboy of 100 or even 50 years ago. The Long
Drive is gone. He goes to roundups in a truck.
Helicopter pilots hovering over the range tell him
by radio where wandering cattle can be found. A
jeep brings a hot lunch from the ranch house.

But the modern cowboy must still know how to ride a horse and sit in the saddle for hours in all kinds of weather. He still must be able to rope a cow and bring it down for branding. He has to be skilled in moving herds of cattle, if not for hundreds of miles, at least to waiting trucks which will take them to railheads, there to be shipped to other areas where they will be fattened on grain.

Perhaps some day machines will be invented
that will rope cows and brand and herd them.
But until that day comes, cowboys will ride
proudly over the range land of the West as they
have done for so many years.

Index